EMMANUEL JOSEPH

Prismatic Pathways, Cultivating Holistic Growth through Time, Health, and Wealth Management

Copyright © 2025 by Emmanuel Joseph

All rights reserved. No part of this publication may be reproduced, stored or transmitted in any form or by any means, electronic, mechanical, photocopying, recording, scanning, or otherwise without written permission from the publisher. It is illegal to copy this book, post it to a website, or distribute it by any other means without permission.

First edition

This book was professionally typeset on Reedsy.
Find out more at reedsy.com

Contents

1	Chapter 1: The Concept of Holistic Growth	1
2	Chapter 2: Mastering Time Management	3
3	Chapter 3: Cultivating Physical Health	5
4	Chapter 4: Nurturing Mental and Emotional Well-being	7
5	Chapter 5: Financial Literacy and Wealth Building	9
6	Chapter 6: Harmonizing Time, Health, and Wealth	11
7	Chapter 7: Building Resilience and Adaptability	13
8	Chapter 8: The Role of Relationships in Holistic Growth	15
9	Chapter 9: The Power of Purpose and Passion	17
10	Chapter 10: Mindfulness and Self-Awareness	19
11	Chapter 11: The Art of Giving and Gratitude	21
12	Chapter 12: Setting Intentions and Manifesting Goals	23
13	Chapter 13: Embracing Change and Growth	25
14	Chapter 14: Creating a Balanced Lifestyle	27
15	Chapter 15: The Journey to Holistic Growth	29

1

Chapter 1: The Concept of Holistic Growth

Holistic growth encompasses nurturing every aspect of our lives, harmonizing time management, health, and wealth to create a balanced and fulfilling existence. This journey begins with an understanding of the interconnectedness of these three elements. Time is a finite resource, and how we allocate it significantly influences our health and wealth. Health, which includes physical, mental, and emotional well-being, is our true wealth. Wealth, in a holistic sense, extends beyond financial stability to include a richness of experiences and opportunities. By aligning these components, we set forth on a prismatic pathway to a meaningful life.

In this chapter, we explore the foundational principles of holistic growth, emphasizing the importance of time management and its impact on our overall well-being. We delve into the necessity of prioritizing self-care and establishing routines that support both physical and mental health. Additionally, we discuss the role of financial literacy and prudent decision-making in achieving a state of wealth that transcends monetary gain. Holistic growth is a continuous journey of self-improvement and balance, where each step we take brings us closer to a harmonious existence.

By understanding the synergy between time, health, and wealth, we can begin to make informed decisions that promote holistic growth. Each component influences the others, and neglecting one aspect can lead to imbalances that hinder overall progress. Therefore, it is crucial to approach our lives with a holistic mindset, recognizing that true growth comes from nurturing every facet of our being. As we embark on this journey, we must remain committed to the principles of balance, mindfulness, and continuous improvement.

Holistic growth is not a destination but a lifelong journey that requires dedication and self-awareness. It involves constantly evaluating our priorities, making adjustments, and seeking opportunities for growth. By embracing this philosophy, we can cultivate a fulfilling and meaningful life that aligns with our values and aspirations. The prismatic pathway to holistic growth is illuminated by our commitment to harmonizing time, health, and wealth.

2

Chapter 2: Mastering Time Management

Effective time management is the cornerstone of holistic growth. Our ability to allocate time wisely determines how well we can nurture our health and build wealth. Time, once lost, cannot be regained, making it crucial to be intentional with its use. By developing time management skills, we create opportunities for self-care, productivity, and financial growth. In this chapter, we explore strategies to master time management and create a well-balanced life.

We begin by identifying common time wasters and how to eliminate them. Procrastination, distractions, and lack of planning are some of the major culprits that hinder our productivity. To counter these, we must cultivate discipline and establish clear priorities. Setting specific, measurable, achievable, relevant, and time-bound (SMART) goals helps us stay focused and on track. By breaking down tasks into smaller, manageable steps, we can make steady progress toward our objectives.

Time-blocking and scheduling are powerful techniques to organize our day efficiently. By allocating specific time slots for different activities, we ensure that each aspect of our lives receives the attention it deserves. This approach helps us maintain a healthy work-life balance and prevents burnout. Additionally, incorporating regular breaks and relaxation periods into our schedule is essential for maintaining mental and physical well-being. Time management is not just about productivity; it is also about ensuring that we have time for rest and rejuvenation.

Mastering time management requires continuous self-assessment and adjustment. We must regularly review our goals, priorities, and schedules to ensure that they align with our values and aspirations. By being flexible and adaptable, we can navigate the challenges and uncertainties of life with confidence. Effective time management empowers us to take control of our lives, enabling us to achieve holistic growth and create a fulfilling existence.

3

Chapter 3: Cultivating Physical Health

Physical health is a vital component of holistic growth. Our bodies are the vessels through which we experience life, and maintaining their well-being is essential. Cultivating physical health involves adopting a balanced diet, engaging in regular exercise, and ensuring adequate rest. In this chapter, we explore the importance of physical health and how to incorporate healthy habits into our daily routine.

A nutritious diet provides the foundation for physical health. Consuming a variety of nutrient-dense foods ensures that our bodies receive the vitamins, minerals, and energy needed to function optimally. Emphasizing whole foods, such as fruits, vegetables, lean proteins, and whole grains, helps us maintain a balanced diet. Additionally, staying hydrated and moderating our intake of processed foods, sugars, and unhealthy fats are crucial for overall well-being. By making mindful food choices, we can support our physical health and prevent chronic diseases.

Regular exercise is essential for maintaining physical health. Engaging in a combination of cardiovascular, strength training, and flexibility exercises helps improve our overall fitness and prevent health issues. Cardiovascular exercises, such as walking, running, or cycling, enhance heart health and increase endurance. Strength training exercises, such as weightlifting or bodyweight exercises, build muscle and improve metabolism. Flexibility exercises, such as yoga or stretching, enhance mobility and reduce the risk of injury. Incorporating a variety of exercises into our routine ensures that we stay fit and healthy.

Adequate rest and sleep are fundamental to physical health. Our bodies need time to recover and repair, and quality sleep plays a crucial role in this process. Establishing a consistent sleep schedule, creating a relaxing bedtime routine, and optimizing our sleep environment are key strategies for improving sleep quality. Additionally, taking regular breaks throughout the day and allowing time for relaxation and leisure activities helps prevent burnout. By prioritizing rest and sleep, we can maintain our physical health and enhance our overall well-being.

4

Chapter 4: Nurturing Mental and Emotional Well-being

Mental and emotional well-being are integral to holistic growth. Our minds and emotions shape our perceptions, decisions, and interactions with the world. Nurturing mental and emotional well-being involves practices such as mindfulness, self-reflection, and seeking support when needed. In this chapter, we delve into strategies to enhance mental and emotional health.

Mindfulness is the practice of being present and fully engaged in the moment. It involves observing our thoughts and feelings without judgment and cultivating a sense of awareness and acceptance. Mindfulness meditation, deep breathing exercises, and mindful activities such as yoga or tai chi are effective ways to practice mindfulness. By incorporating mindfulness into our daily routine, we can reduce stress, improve focus, and enhance our overall well-being. Mindfulness helps us develop a deeper connection with ourselves and the world around us.

Self-reflection and journaling are powerful tools for nurturing mental and emotional well-being. Taking time to reflect on our thoughts, feelings, and experiences helps us gain insights into our inner world. Journaling allows us to express our emotions, process our thoughts, and identify patterns and triggers. By regularly engaging in self-reflection and journaling, we can enhance our self-awareness, develop emotional intelligence, and foster personal growth. These practices provide a safe space for introspection and self-discovery.

Seeking support from friends, family, or professionals is crucial for maintaining mental and emotional well-being. Building a strong support network provides us with emotional nourishment, encouragement, and guidance. Talking to trusted individuals about our struggles and seeking advice or therapy when needed can help us navigate challenges and build resilience. Additionally, engaging in social activities and cultivating positive relationships contribute to our emotional well-being. By seeking support and fostering connections, we can enhance our mental and emotional health.

5

Chapter 5: Financial Literacy and Wealth Building

Financial literacy is a crucial aspect of holistic growth. Understanding how to manage finances, invest wisely, and plan for the future empowers us to build wealth. Wealth is not just about accumulating money but also creating a stable and fulfilling life. In this chapter, we explore the principles of financial literacy and strategies for wealth building.

Budgeting is the foundation of financial literacy. It involves tracking our income, expenses, and savings to ensure that we live within our means and allocate resources effectively. Creating a budget helps us identify spending patterns, prioritize financial goals, and make informed decisions. By setting aside a portion of our income for savings and investments, we can build a financial cushion for emergencies and future needs. Budgeting is a proactive approach to managing our finances and achieving financial stability.

Investing is a powerful tool for wealth building. By investing in assets such as stocks, bonds, real estate, or mutual funds, we can grow our wealth over time. Understanding the principles of risk and return, diversification, and long-term planning is essential for successful investing. Additionally, seeking professional advice and staying informed about market trends and economic factors can help us make wise investment decisions. Investing allows us to create passive income streams and build a financial foundation for future growth.

Planning for retirement is a key aspect of wealth building. Ensuring that we have adequate savings and investments to support our lifestyle in retirement requires careful planning and disciplined saving. Contributing to retirement accounts, such as 401(k)s or IRAs, and taking advantage of employer-sponsored retirement plans are effective strategies. Additionally, considering factors such as healthcare costs, inflation, and potential changes in income is crucial for a comprehensive retirement plan. By planning for retirement, we can achieve financial security and enjoy a fulfilling post-work life.

6

Chapter 6: Harmonizing Time, Health, and Wealth

Harmonizing time, health, and wealth is the essence of holistic growth. These three elements are interconnected, and their balance is crucial for a fulfilling life. In this chapter, we explore how to integrate time management, health practices, and financial strategies to create a harmonious existence.

Setting holistic goals that encompass time, health, and wealth is essential. We must identify our priorities and create a balanced approach to achieving them. For example, setting goals that include regular exercise, healthy eating, financial savings, and personal development helps us maintain balance. Creating daily routines that support these goals ensures that each aspect of our lives receives the attention it deserves. Additionally, incorporating flexibility into our plans allows us to adapt to changing circumstances and stay on track.

To harmonize time, health, and wealth, we must regularly assess and adjust our priorities. Life is dynamic, and our needs and goals may evolve over time. By conducting periodic self-assessments, we can identify areas that require attention and make necessary adjustments. This process helps us stay aligned with our holistic growth objectives and ensures that we maintain balance. Embracing change and being open to new opportunities are key to achieving harmony in our lives.

Building a supportive environment is also crucial for harmonizing time, health, and wealth. Surrounding ourselves with like-minded individuals who share our values and goals fosters a sense of community and encouragement. Engaging in activities that promote well-being, such as group exercises, financial workshops, or wellness retreats, enhances our overall growth. By fostering a supportive network, we create a positive atmosphere that nurtures holistic growth and empowers us to thrive.

Chapter 7: Building Resilience and Adaptability

Resilience and adaptability are essential qualities for holistic growth. Life is unpredictable, and our ability to bounce back from challenges and adapt to change determines our progress. In this chapter, we explore strategies to build resilience and adaptability.

Developing a growth mindset is crucial for resilience. By viewing challenges as opportunities for growth and learning, we can shift our perspective and build mental and emotional strength. Techniques such as positive self-talk, visualization, and affirmations help cultivate a growth mindset. Embracing failure as a learning experience and celebrating small victories further reinforces our resilience. A growth mindset empowers us to face adversity with confidence and determination.

Building mental and emotional resilience involves developing coping strategies to manage stress and adversity. Practices such as mindfulness meditation, deep breathing exercises, and progressive muscle relaxation help reduce stress and promote emotional well-being. Additionally, engaging in activities that bring joy and fulfillment, such as hobbies, socializing, or volunteering, enhances our emotional resilience. By nurturing our mental and emotional health, we build a solid foundation for resilience and adaptability.

Adaptability requires us to be flexible and open to change. Embracing uncertainty and being willing to adjust our plans and goals allows us to navigate life's twists and turns. Developing problem-solving skills and staying informed about new trends and opportunities helps us adapt to changing circumstances. Additionally, seeking feedback and learning from others' experiences enhances our adaptability. By being open to change and continuously seeking improvement, we can thrive in an ever-evolving world.

Resilience and adaptability are qualities that can be cultivated over time. By consistently practicing strategies to build mental, emotional, and physical strength, we can enhance our ability to face challenges and seize opportunities. These qualities are essential for holistic growth, enabling us to navigate life's journey with confidence and grace. Embracing resilience and adaptability empowers us to achieve our goals and create a fulfilling and balanced life.

8

Chapter 8: The Role of Relationships in Holistic Growth

Relationships play a significant role in holistic growth. Our connections with others influence our mental, emotional, and even physical well-being. In this chapter, we explore the importance of cultivating healthy relationships and building a supportive network.

Healthy relationships are based on qualities such as trust, respect, and empathy. Effective communication and active listening are essential for fostering strong connections. By being present and attentive in our interactions, we build trust and understanding with others. Setting boundaries and prioritizing self-care within relationships ensure that they remain balanced and nurturing. By cultivating these qualities, we create relationships that contribute to our holistic growth.

Building a supportive network involves surrounding ourselves with individuals who share our values and goals. Engaging in activities and communities that align with our interests fosters a sense of belonging and support. Joining groups, clubs, or organizations related to our passions provides opportunities to connect with like-minded individuals. Additionally, seeking mentorship and guidance from those with experience and wisdom enhances our growth. A supportive network empowers us to achieve our goals and navigate challenges with confidence.

Nurturing relationships requires effort and commitment. Regularly connecting with loved ones, expressing appreciation, and offering support strengthen our bonds. Engaging in meaningful conversations and shared activities fosters deeper connections. Additionally, being open to feedback and willing to resolve conflicts constructively enhances our relationships. By prioritizing the well-being of our relationships, we create a positive and supportive environment that contributes to our holistic growth.

Relationships are a vital component of our holistic growth journey. They provide emotional nourishment, encouragement, and guidance, enriching our lives and contributing to our overall well-being. By cultivating healthy relationships and building a supportive network, we create a strong foundation for personal growth and fulfillment. The role of relationships in holistic growth cannot be underestimated, as they are the threads that weave the fabric of our lives.

9

Chapter 9: The Power of Purpose and Passion

Purpose and passion drive our actions and give meaning to our lives. Identifying and pursuing our passions and aligning them with our purpose is key to holistic growth. In this chapter, we explore how to discover our purpose and ignite our passions.

Self-discovery involves exploring our interests, values, and strengths. Taking time to reflect on what brings us joy and fulfillment helps us identify our passions. Techniques such as journaling, meditation, and seeking feedback from trusted individuals can provide insights into our core values and aspirations. By gaining clarity on our purpose, we can align our actions with our true calling and pursue a fulfilling life.

Pursuing our passions with dedication and enthusiasm ignites a sense of purpose and motivation. Setting meaningful goals and creating a plan of action helps us stay focused and on track. Embracing challenges and learning from failures further fuels our passion and resilience. By dedicating time and energy to our passions, we create a sense of fulfillment and joy that enhances our overall well-being. Pursuing our passions allows us to live authentically and purposefully.

Aligning our passions with our purpose involves integrating them into different aspects of our lives. Whether through our careers, hobbies, or volunteer work, we can find ways to express our passions and make a positive impact. By aligning our actions with our values, we create a sense of coherence and harmony in our lives. This alignment fosters a sense of meaning and purpose, driving us to achieve our goals and contribute to the greater good. Living in alignment with our purpose brings a sense of fulfillment and satisfaction.

Purpose and passion are powerful forces that drive holistic growth. They provide direction, motivation, and a sense of meaning, empowering us to pursue our dreams and create a fulfilling life. By embracing our purpose and igniting our passions, we can cultivate a life that is rich with joy, fulfillment, and growth. The power of purpose and passion lies in their ability to transform our lives and guide us on the prismatic pathway to holistic growth.

10

Chapter 10: Mindfulness and Self-Awareness

Mindfulness and self-awareness are essential for holistic growth. Being present in the moment and understanding ourselves allows us to make conscious decisions that align with our goals. In this chapter, we explore practices to cultivate mindfulness and self-awareness.

Mindfulness involves being fully present and engaged in the current moment, without judgment. This practice helps us become more aware of our thoughts, feelings, and surroundings. Mindfulness meditation, deep breathing exercises, and mindful activities such as yoga or tai chi are effective ways to practice mindfulness. By incorporating mindfulness into our daily routine, we can reduce stress, improve focus, and enhance our overall well-being. Mindfulness helps us develop a deeper connection with ourselves and the world around us.

Self-awareness involves gaining insights into our thoughts, emotions, and behaviors. Self-reflection and journaling are powerful tools for enhancing self-awareness. By regularly reflecting on our experiences and writing down our thoughts and feelings, we can identify patterns and triggers. This process helps us understand our strengths, weaknesses, and areas for growth. Self-awareness enables us to make conscious decisions that align with our values and goals, fostering personal growth and emotional intelligence.

Being present in our interactions and activities fosters deeper connections and a sense of fulfillment. When we are fully engaged in our conversations and activities, we build stronger relationships and create meaningful experiences. Practicing active listening and being attentive to others' needs and feelings enhances our social connections. Additionally, being present in our work and hobbies increases our productivity and satisfaction. By cultivating mindfulness and self-awareness, we create a balanced and fulfilling life.

Mindfulness and self-awareness are continuous practices that require dedication and effort. By consistently engaging in mindfulness activities and self-reflection, we can enhance our well-being and personal growth. These practices enable us to live intentionally and authentically, fostering a deeper connection with ourselves and the world around us. The journey to holistic growth is illuminated by our commitment to mindfulness and self-awareness.

11

Chapter 11: The Art of Giving and Gratitude

Giving and gratitude are powerful practices that enhance holistic growth. Acts of kindness and expressing gratitude create positive energy and strengthen our connections with others. In this chapter, we explore the impact of giving and gratitude on our well-being.

Giving fosters a sense of purpose and fulfillment. Whether through acts of kindness, volunteering, or philanthropy, giving allows us to make a positive impact on others' lives. The act of giving creates a sense of connection and empathy, enhancing our relationships and social well-being. Additionally, giving can improve our mental and emotional health by fostering feelings of joy and satisfaction. By incorporating giving into our lives, we can create a ripple effect of positivity and well-being.

Gratitude involves appreciating the positive aspects of our lives and expressing thanks for them. Practicing gratitude enhances our mental and emotional health by promoting a positive mindset. Techniques such as gratitude journaling, where we write down things we are grateful for each day, help us cultivate an attitude of gratitude. Expressing gratitude to others, whether through words or actions, strengthens our relationships and fosters a sense of connection. By regularly practicing gratitude, we can improve our overall well-being and create a positive outlook on life.

Creating a culture of giving and gratitude within our communities fosters a sense of unity and support. Engaging in community service, supporting local charities, and participating in group activities that promote kindness and gratitude help build a positive environment. By encouraging others to practice giving and gratitude, we create a collective impact that enhances the well-being of our communities. The art of giving and gratitude enriches our lives and fosters a sense of belonging and purpose.

Giving and gratitude are practices that can be cultivated and integrated into our daily lives. By consistently engaging in acts of kindness and expressing appreciation, we can enhance our well-being and foster holistic growth. These practices create a positive mindset and strengthen our connections with others, contributing to a fulfilling and meaningful life. The art of giving and gratitude is a powerful force that illuminates the prismatic pathway to holistic growth.

12

Chapter 12: Setting Intentions and Manifesting Goals

Setting intentions and manifesting goals are essential steps in achieving holistic growth. Intentions provide direction, and focused action brings our goals to fruition. In this chapter, we explore how to set clear intentions and manifest our desired outcomes.

Intentions provide a sense of purpose and direction in our lives. By setting clear and meaningful intentions, we create a roadmap for our actions and decisions. Techniques such as visualization, where we imagine ourselves achieving our goals, help clarify our intentions. Writing down our intentions and reviewing them regularly keeps us focused and motivated. By setting intentions, we can align our actions with our values and create a sense of purpose and fulfillment.

SMART (Specific, Measurable, Achievable, Relevant, Time-bound) goals provide a structured approach to achieving our intentions. Breaking down our goals into smaller, manageable steps makes them more achievable and less overwhelming. Creating an action plan with specific tasks and deadlines helps us stay organized and on track. Additionally, regularly reviewing and adjusting our goals ensures that they remain relevant and aligned with our values. By setting SMART goals, we can take deliberate actions that lead to the manifestation of our desires.

Perseverance and adaptability are key to overcoming obstacles and staying on track. The journey to achieving our goals may be filled with challenges and setbacks, but maintaining a positive mindset and staying committed to our intentions helps us navigate these difficulties. Being open to change and willing to adjust our plans as needed ensures that we remain flexible and adaptable. By embracing perseverance and adaptability, we can stay focused on our goals and achieve holistic growth.

Manifesting goals involves taking consistent and focused action towards our desired outcomes. By regularly reviewing our intentions, setting SMART goals, and taking deliberate actions, we can bring our dreams to life. The process of manifesting goals requires dedication, effort, and a positive mindset. By staying committed to our intentions and taking proactive steps, we can achieve our goals and create a fulfilling and meaningful life. Setting intentions and manifesting goals are powerful practices that illuminate the prismatic pathway to holistic growth.

13

Chapter 13: Embracing Change and Growth

      Change and growth are constants in life, and embracing them is crucial for holistic growth. Our ability to adapt to change and continuously seek self-improvement determines our progress. In this chapter, we explore strategies to embrace change and foster growth.

Having a positive attitude towards change enables us to see opportunities rather than obstacles. By viewing change as a natural part of life, we can shift our perspective and embrace it with an open mind. Techniques such as reframing, where we look for the positive aspects of a situation, help us develop a positive attitude towards change. Embracing change with a growth mindset allows us to see challenges as opportunities for learning and development. A positive attitude towards change empowers us to navigate life's transitions with confidence and resilience.

Developing resilience and adaptability is essential for embracing change. Resilience involves bouncing back from setbacks and challenges with strength and determination. Techniques such as positive self-talk, visualization, and stress management help build resilience. Adaptability requires us to be flexible and open to new experiences and ideas. By staying informed about new trends and opportunities, seeking feedback, and being willing to adjust our plans, we can enhance our adaptability. Resilience and adaptability enable us to navigate change and seize opportunities for growth.

Lifelong learning and personal development are key components of embracing change and growth. By continuously seeking new knowledge and skills, we can stay relevant and adaptable in a rapidly changing world. Engaging in activities such as reading, taking courses, attending workshops, and seeking mentorship fosters personal and professional growth. Additionally, being open to feedback and willing to learn from our experiences enhances our development. Lifelong learning and personal development empower us to achieve our goals and create a fulfilling life.

Embracing change and growth is a continuous journey that requires dedication and effort. By maintaining a positive attitude, building resilience and adaptability, and seeking lifelong learning and personal development, we can navigate life's transitions with confidence and grace. These strategies enable us to embrace change as an opportunity for growth and create a fulfilling and balanced life. Embracing change and growth is essential for holistic growth, empowering us to achieve our goals and live a meaningful life.

14

Chapter 14: Creating a Balanced Lifestyle

Creating a balanced lifestyle is the culmination of holistic growth. It involves harmonizing our time, health, and wealth to create a fulfilling existence. In this chapter, we explore how to create and maintain a balanced lifestyle.

Setting priorities and creating routines that support balance are essential. Identifying our core values and aligning our actions with them helps us maintain focus and direction. Creating daily and weekly routines that incorporate time for work, self-care, and leisure ensures that each aspect of our lives receives attention. Additionally, being mindful of our energy levels and setting realistic expectations helps prevent burnout. By setting priorities and creating routines, we can maintain a balanced lifestyle that supports holistic growth.

Managing stress and preventing burnout are crucial for maintaining balance. Techniques such as mindfulness meditation, deep breathing exercises, and progressive muscle relaxation help reduce stress and promote relaxation. Additionally, engaging in activities that bring joy and fulfillment, such as hobbies, socializing, or spending time in nature, enhances our well-being. Setting boundaries and learning to say no when necessary helps prevent overcommitment and burnout. By managing stress and preventing burnout, we can maintain our physical, mental, and emotional health.

Regular self-assessment and adjustment ensure that we stay on track. Life is dynamic, and our needs and goals may evolve over time. By conducting periodic self-assessments, we can identify areas that require attention and make necessary adjustments. This process helps us stay aligned with our holistic growth objectives and ensures that we maintain balance. Embracing change and being open to new opportunities are key to achieving a balanced lifestyle. Regular self-assessment and adjustment empower us to navigate life's transitions and maintain balance.

Creating a balanced lifestyle involves continuous effort and commitment. By setting priorities, managing stress, and regularly assessing our progress, we can create a fulfilling and balanced existence. A balanced lifestyle supports holistic growth and enables us to thrive in every aspect of our lives. By embracing balance, we create a harmonious and meaningful life that aligns with our values and aspirations.

15

Chapter 15: The Journey to Holistic Growth

Holistic growth is a continuous journey of self-improvement and balance. It involves integrating time management, health practices, and financial strategies to create a fulfilling life. In this final chapter, we reflect on the journey to holistic growth and offer practical tips for staying on the prismatic pathway.

Holistic growth requires a commitment to self-awareness and continuous improvement. By regularly reflecting on our progress and making adjustments, we can ensure that we stay aligned with our goals and values. Embracing a growth mindset, where we see challenges as opportunities for learning and development, empowers us to navigate life's ups and downs with resilience and confidence. The journey to holistic growth is not a destination but a lifelong commitment to personal and collective well-being.

Building a supportive community is essential for holistic growth. Surrounding ourselves with like-minded individuals who share our values and goals creates a sense of connection and encouragement. Engaging in activities that promote well-being, such as group exercises, financial workshops, or wellness retreats, enhances our overall growth. By fostering a supportive network, we create a positive environment that nurtures holistic growth and empowers us to thrive.

Practicing gratitude and giving back to others enriches our journey to holistic growth. By appreciating the positive aspects of our lives and expressing gratitude, we create a positive mindset that enhances our well-being. Acts of kindness and giving back to our communities foster a sense of purpose and fulfillment. By incorporating gratitude and giving into our lives, we create a ripple effect of positivity and well-being. These practices contribute to our holistic growth and create a sense of belonging and purpose.

The journey to holistic growth is illuminated by our commitment to harmonizing time, health, and wealth. By embracing mindfulness, self-awareness, resilience, and adaptability, we create a fulfilling and balanced life. The prismatic pathway to holistic growth is a lifelong journey of self-improvement, balance, and meaningful connections. By staying committed to our values and continuously seeking growth, we can create a harmonious and fulfilling life that aligns with our aspirations.

Book Description

Prismatic Pathways: Cultivating Holistic Growth through Time, Health, and Wealth Management is a comprehensive guide to achieving a balanced and fulfilling life. This book explores the interconnectedness of time management, health, and wealth, and offers practical strategies for integrating these elements to create holistic growth. Through fifteen insightful chapters, readers will discover the principles of effective time management, the importance of physical and mental well-being, and the key aspects of financial literacy and wealth building.

The book emphasizes the importance of setting holistic goals, building resilience, nurturing relationships, and embracing change. It provides practical tips for creating a balanced lifestyle, managing stress, and cultivating a positive mindset. With a focus on mindfulness, self-awareness, and continuous improvement, **Prismatic Pathways** empowers readers to navigate life's journey with confidence and grace.

Whether you are seeking personal growth, financial stability, or overall well-being, this book offers valuable insights and actionable steps to guide you on the prismatic pathway to holistic growth. Embrace the journey to a harmonious and meaningful life with **Prismatic Pathways** as your

CHAPTER 15: THE JOURNEY TO HOLISTIC GROWTH

companion.

www.ingramcontent.com/pod-product-compliance
Lightning Source LLC
LaVergne TN
LVHW020502080526
838202LV00057B/6112